970.01   Barden, Renardo
BAR
          The discovery of
          America

$13.95

GREAT MYSTERIES

The Discovery of America

OPPOSING VIEWPOINTS®

Look for these and other exciting *Great Mysteries:
Opposing Viewpoints* books:

GREAT MYSTERIES
The Discovery of America
OPPOSING VIEWPOINTS®

by Renardo Barden

Greenhaven Press, Inc.   P.O. Box 289009, San Diego, California 92128-9009

Library of Congress Cataloging-in-Publication Data

Barden, Renardo.
    The discovery of America.

    (Great mysteries : opposing viewpoints)
    Bibliography: p.
    Includes index
    Summary: Explores the question of who was the first European to set foot on American soil. Columbus? Vikings? Others?
    1. America—Discovery and exploration—Pre-Columbian—Juvenile literature. [1. America—Discovery and exploration—Pre-Columbian] I. Title. II Series: Great mysteries (Saint Paul, Minn.)
E103.B36   1989   970.01'1   89-11709
ISBN 0-89908-071-5

© Copyright 1989 by Greenhaven Press, Inc.
Produced by Carnival Enterprises, Minneapolis, MN
Every effort has been made to trace owners of copyright material.

Like Columbus, Brendan, Madoc, Karlsefni
and the adventurers in this book,
he's a dreamer, an explorer, and a navigator;
this book is for my son Michael.

*Facts do not penetrate into the world where our beliefs live,
and since they do not give them birth, they cannot kill them;
and a torrent of misfortunes or illnesses which, one after the other
afflict a family, will not make it doubt in the goodness of its God
and the skills of its physician.*

—Marcel Proust

Contents

Introduction

This book is written for the curious—those who want to explore the mysteries that are everywhere. To be human is to be constantly surrounded by wonderment. How do birds fly? Are ghosts real? Can animals and people communicate? Was King Arthur a real person or a myth? Why did Amelia Earhart disappear? Did history really happen the way we think it did? Where did the world come from? Where is it going?

Great Mysteries: Opposing Viewpoints books are intended to offer the reader an opportunity to explore some of the many mysteries that both trouble and intrigue us. For the span of each book, we want the reader to feel that he or she is a scientist investigating the extinction of the dinosaurs, an archaeologist searching for clues to the origin of the great Egyptian pyramids, a psychic detective testing the existence of ESP.

One thing all mysteries have in common is that there is no ready answer. Often there are *many* answers but none on which even the majority of authorities agrees. *Great Mysteries: Opposing Viewpoints* books introduce the intriguing views of the experts, allowing the reader to participate in their explorations, their theories, and their disagreements as they try to explain the mysteries of our world.

But most readers won't want to stop here. These *Great Mysteries: Opposing Viewpoints* aim to stimulate the reader's curiosity. Although truth is often impossible to discover, the search is fascinating. It is up to the reader to examine the evidence, to decide whether the answer is there—or to explore further.

"Penetrating so many secrets, we cease to believe in the unknowable. But there it sits nevertheless, calmly licking its chops."
H.L. Mencken, American essayist

One

Is the Discovery of America a Mystery?

Early in October, with his men afraid of sailing off the edge of the world and threatening to mutiny, Christopher Columbus struck a bargain with his crew. He asked them for three more days and promised to turn back toward Spain if at the end of that time no land was yet in sight. He reminded them, too, that the king and queen of Spain had promised an annual pension to the man who first spotted land. It was to be Columbus himself who claimed the pension. Shortly before 10:00 at night on October 12, 1492, Columbus wrote that he saw "a little wax candle rising and falling."

As it turned out, this "candle" was the dawning flicker of a new age. Columbus had arrived in the New World and the old world would never be the same.

Calendars list October 12 as Columbus Day. History and geography teachers tell us that Christopher Columbus landed in the New World on that date. Many workers are given the day off. So it is reasonable to wonder just how and why the discovery of America qualifies as a historical mystery. Why cannot we just accept that Columbus discovered America and leave it at that?

Opposite page: the man whose name we honor every October 12—Christopher Columbus. Was he truly the first European to visit the New World?

Columbus' expedition landed on the island of San Salvador, in the Caribbean.

Actually, Columbus did not discover the United States or even the continents of North or South America. He landed in the Bahamas on the island of San Salvador. But he sailed unknown waters, braving the west Atlantic Ocean and daring what no man had dared before him. The natives of San Salvador told him of other islands where he would find the spices and gold both he and all of Europe craved. On this, his first of four voyages, Columbus discovered the first islands that were like links in a chain. As one island led to another, Columbus and those who followed him arrived on the shores of the American continents. While few dispute the importance of Columbus' arrival in San Salvador, there is some evidence that Columbus was not the first voyager to set foot in these new lands.

Until little over a hundred years ago, historians largely ignored Norwegian claims that their ancestors, the Vikings, had landed in North America some five hundred years before Columbus. Since that time, discoveries of abandoned settlements in Greenland and North America have turned up important evidence that requires the Viking claims be taken more seriously. This demonstrates that historians are always rewriting history so it continues to reflect what we are discovering about the past. History is not just an unchanging set of facts. It is a process.

Columbus and his voyage to America are one example of this process. We can and ought to admire Columbus for his vision and boldness. But new discoveries and changing viewpoints require that we reevaluate his 1492 adventure. In a way, our confusion about the Columbus discovery might be said to go back a long, long time.

Where Did Native Americans Come From?

About 40,000 years ago, several centuries of frigid weather caused gigantic glaciers to form over most of the land in the northern hemisphere. This Ice Age lowered the water level of the world's oceans. The islands that now dot the Bering Strait between Alaska and eastern Asia became a continuous land bridge known as Beringia. This bridge enabled Asians to walk to the Americas.

According to evidence gathered by anthropologists, North America was discovered by the men, women, and children who first wandered eastward out of Asia. Therefore, any discussion of the discovery of America owes a tribute to these hardy people.

Some of these "Beringians" stayed in the north, occupying the lands that today we call Alaska and Canada. Others moved south, winding up in the present-day countries of the United States, Mexico, and Central and South America.

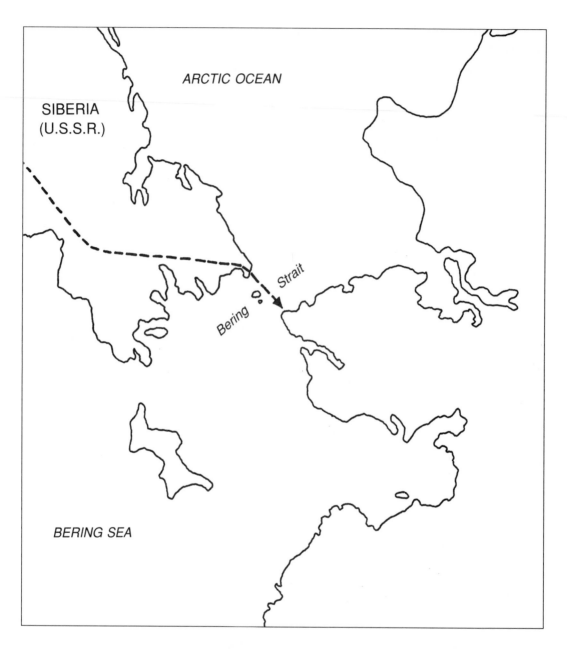

The Bering Strait separates Asia and North America, but long ago animals and people crossed freely when no water covered this "land bridge." The Native Americans who Columbus found had been in the Western Hemisphere for thousands of years.

The oldest crude tools made by these wanderers have been found to be between 20,000 and 27,000 years old. But some human skulls recently unearthed on the west coast may be even older, suggesting that the first immigrants might have reached present-day California as much as 40,000 years ago. In another sense, though, the Beringians didn't so much discover America as arrive here.

Discovery or Brutal Invasion?

What we think of as the discovery of America is partly the story of a clash of cultures that caused changes—in the way Native Americans lived, and in the way later settlers would live. Tragically, many of these changes were destructive beyond belief. The Spaniards, for instance, completely destroyed the ancient civilizations of the Aztecs of Mexico and the Inca of Peru. Slavery, violence, new diseases (against which the natives had no natural resistance), and destruction of agricultural lands brought about enormous suffering.

Modern historians estimate that in their first fifty years in the New World the Spanish directly or indirectly brought about the deaths of as many as 20 million Native Americans. Surprisingly, until a few years ago, these tragic facts were downplayed or scarcely mentioned in American history books. The truths of history have a way of remaining hidden for a long time, and historians are left with the task of connecting known facts to things that probably happened. This takes some intelligent speculation—or simply put, guesswork.

This is so because reliable information is always hard to come by. Sometimes, historical records are unclear, unwritten, conflicting, or confusing. But even so, record keeping societies are subject to fires, floods, earthquakes, thefts, and wars. The plundering and pillaging of cities once at the heart of civilization has resulted in the loss of historically important

Montezuma, king of the great Aztec civilization of Mexico.

information—just how much we shall never know.

But personal motives have probably been even more destructive to historical truth than wars and disasters. In order to be well thought of—not only by their contemporaries, but by generations to come—many leaders and governments have falsified reports of events. Some want to evade responsibility for the bad things they have caused. Others seek the credit for the good things actually done by others.

Of course, not all history is cloaked in deliberate

The Aztec city of Teotihuacan was taken by the Spanish explorer Cortez in 1519 in one of the most devastating blows to Native American culture.

The great artistry of the Mesoamerican world was virtually destroyed by the invasion of European culture. Shown here is a funeral urn from the province of Oaxaca, Mexico, dating from the thirteenth century.

deceit. Some of it is simple. We can learn easily enough that the Yankees won the World Series in 1937 by defeating the Giants in five games. Not only are there men and women alive who attended the games, but newspaper stories, film footage, and radio broadcast tapes are also available.

The discovery of America, however, was not so well documented. And since the day Columbus returned to Spain from his first voyage, people have asked difficult questions about the importance of his discovery. With the passage of time, those questions have increased in number. What, precisely, are these questions?

Few would deny that in 1492 a man named Christopher Columbus went ashore on the island of San Salvador, claiming it on behalf of Ferdinand and Isabella, the King and Queen of Spain. They supported his expedition and saw to it that he would have three small ships for the voyage. We have a strong consensus about the basic facts of this important event.

But efforts to influence history and devalue the importance of Columbus' 1492 voyage began almost immediately after he returned to Spain the following year. Beginning then and continuing into our own times, facts about Columbus have been challenged again and again. For instance, though Columbus said he came from Genoa, a city in Italy, others have

This calendar, carved in stone, was another Aztec achievement nearly erased by the Spanish conquistadors and their priests.

The Vikings, the renowned conquering seamen of Europe, told of their travels
to a vast continent in the West called Vinland.

argued that he was Spanish, Portuguese, English, French, or Greek. Though he wrote and spoke of his devout Christian faith, some have claimed he was Jewish. Now while these disputes may not shed light on who did or did not discover America, they are important, because they directly attack our faith in the written records of those days. If, for example, a historian who said that Columbus was born in Genoa turned out to be wrong, we would begin to doubt other claims made by that historian.

There are more important areas of confusion touching on his famous voyage. Do we really mean to insist, for example, that Columbus discovered America? Not really, since to do so is to dismiss the fact that it was already occupied. The famous navigator met Native Americans on his very first day on the island of San Salvador. At the same time, even as Columbus "discovered" America, the city of Teotihuacan (which had once housed as many as 250,000 people) stood abandoned in the sun and winds of central Mexico. What happened to the inhabitants of this city that had once been one of the largest in the world? We do not really know. It is one of many mysteries about early America.

What Exactly Do We Mean by America?

Often we who call ourselves Americans arrogantly think that "America" is limited to the United States of America. Columbus voyaged to many islands in the Caribbean, landed briefly in Panama and sailed south until he came to the mouth of the Orinoco River in South America. But he never set foot in the present-day United States.

Another Italian, a Florentine named Amerigo Vespucci, sailed down the east coast of South America. When he returned to Spain he drew a map of the South American coastline. He wrote so compellingly of this New World that the new lands found by Columbus were ultimately named after Amerigo.

"The bearer of this, Amerigo Vespucci, is going there to the court where he has been summoned in connection with matters of navigation; it has always been his desire to give me pleasure; he is a man of goodwill....He is acting on my behalf, moved by a great desire to do something which shall be to my benefit if it lies within his power."

Christopher Columbus, from a letter to his son Diego

"Strange that broad America must wear the name of a thief. Amerigo Vespucci, the pickle dealer at Seville... whose highest naval rank was boatswain's mate in an expedition that never sailed, managed in this lying world to supplant Columbus and baptize half the earth with his own dishonest name."

Ralph Waldo Emerson, American philosopher, 1856

Leif Erikson is believed to be the first Viking leader to set foot on the North American continent.

And what of the claims that other men preceded Columbus to the New World? According to a series of old manuscripts known as the *Icelandic Sagas,* around the year A.D. 1000, a few daring Norwegian explorers known as Vikings were blown south and west of Greenland and happened on the shores of North America—a land they called Vinland. The sagas tell us that the Vikings even attempted to colonize this new land.

There are those who believe the Welsh arrived before the Vikings. Still other historians insist the Irish were in America before the Welsh. Some even argue that Phoenicians, Egyptians, Minoans, and others may well have voyaged across the Atlantic before the time of Christ.

In the chapters that follow, we will examine the Columbus claim of discovering America in light of the *Icelandic Sagas* that tell of men and women who landed in a place they called Vinland. And we will discuss the claims that others were here even before the Vikings.

Two

Did Columbus Discover America?

Columbus spent much of the first forty years of his life in drudgery, daydreams, poverty, and waiting— waiting for his big chance—to seek the ocean route to the Indies by sailing west across the Atlantic Ocean. His conviction that he could and would discover a route to Asia never flagged. In fact, even at the end of his life his belief in his mission was so strong that long after another person would have admitted that he had discovered some new land and not Asia, Columbus refused to consider it.

Though almost every aspect of Columbus' early life has been disputed by someone, our concern here is less with his origins and earlier voyages than with his four trips across the Atlantic. The generally accepted biographical facts are these:

Christoforo Colombo, whom we know as Christopher Columbus, was born in about 1451 to poor parents in Genoa, in what is now a city in northwest Italy. He was the eldest of three surviving sons. His father, Domenico Columbo, was a weaver. Ill-suited to practice his father's trade, Christopher went to sea as soon as he could make himself useful.

"At a very tender age," he wrote to the King and

TERRE. DU CAP DE BONE ESPERANSE

Cap de bonne esperance

MER OCEANE.

TERRE AUSTRAL

"Christoforo Columbo was a young Genoese whose Italian was not presentable, and whose culture-language was Spanish....Now there is only one reasonable way of explaining this fact: The Columbo family were Spanish Jews settled in Genoa, who following the traditions of their race, had remained faithful to the language of their country of origin."

Salvador De Madariaga, *Christopher Columbus*

"Every contemporary Spaniard or Portuguese who wrote about Columbus and his discoveries calls him a Genoese. Four contemporary Genoese chroniclers claim him as a compatriot. Nobody in his lifetime, or for three centuries after, had any doubt about his origin or birthplace."

Samuel Eliot Morison, *The European Discovery of America*

Queen of Spain toward the end of his life, "I entered the life of a sailor and have continued to this day...Already forty years have passed that I have been in this employment."

In 1476, Columbus was aboard a Genoese cargo ship when it was attacked off the coast of Portugal by a French and Portuguese war fleet. The ship on which Columbus was sailing sank, and many lives were lost. Columbus survived, swimming six miles to the shores of Portugal.

Portugal, the country where he spent the next several years of his life, was an exciting place. Portuguese ships were among the best, and they were sailed by some of the boldest men in Europe. For a time, Columbus worked as a mapmaker. He married Dona Felipa Perestrello e Moniz, a woman who belonged to one of the most important and influential families in Portugal. This marriage enabled Columbus to gain the ear of King John II of Portugal. With the help of family connections, Columbus initially sought John's support in 1484 for his proposed westward voyage.

King John was not persuaded, however. Like other worldly men of his time, John had heard the theory that the world was round. Columbus claimed that the Indies—a land said to be rich in gold, spices, and all the things Europeans wanted and lacked— could be reached by sailing westward. King John was willing to admit this. But finding a route to the Indies by rounding the Cape of Good Hope in Africa appeared a surer thing to him. And he already had navigators like Bartholomew Dias searching for just such a route.

When it became clear that John would not support his enterprise, Columbus journeyed to Spain. There he appealed to King Ferdinand and Queen Isabella. Isabella was particularly sympathetic to Columbus' vision, the more so when he talked to her of the millions of souls that might become baptized

Christians. The king and queen were so attracted to his ideas that they granted him an allowance, enabling him to stay in Spain and remain in close contact with the court.

Columbus Gains Spanish Support

When, in early 1492, the city of Granada became the last city in Spain to be liberated from the Islamic Moors, Isabella and Ferdinand felt free to consider the navigator's dream of finding a western route to the Indies. The rival Portuguese had finally rounded the southern tip of Africa and seemed ready to begin a profitable trade with the Indies. This made Columbus' voyage all the more important to Spain.

At last, Ferdinand and Isabella agreed to Columbus' rather demanding conditions. They granted him a very large share of any riches he might discover, and they made him an Admiral. They declared he would be the Viceroy (a governor) of any new lands he happened upon.

On August 3, 1492, he and a crew of about 100 men set sail from the town of Palos in Spain in *The Niña, The Pinta, and The Santa María*, stopping over in the Canary Islands off the coast of West Africa. From those islands, after an anxious six-week voyage, the three ships arrived at San Salvador in the Bahamas on October 12, 1492.

Later, while exploring the Caribbean, *The Santa María* was driven onto a reef off the coast of Haiti, obliging Columbus to leave many of his men behind in a settlement he dubbed La Natividad.

Columbus took several natives back to Europe with him, as well as some parrots, a few gold trinkets, and other exotic items from the New World. More important than these goods, however, was the promise of gold and spices and making converts to the Christian faith. The future seemed too good to be true.

For Columbus the good future never arrived.

The ships of Columbus set sail on August 3, 1492, bound to find a western trade route to the collection of Asian islands known to Europeans as the "Indies."

On his first return to Spain, Columbus was given a hero's welcome and days of parades and feasting. He spent long hours regaling the King and Queen with stories and promises of the gold he would find and the Christian converts he would make. Unfortunately, this did not happen. Before his life was over, the court would come to regard him as a pest.

Short-Lived Success

Honored though he was by the King and Queen, Columbus did not tarry long in Spain. Within five months, he set sail once again with seventeen vessels and about twelve hundred men. He hoped, of course, that his New World colony of La Natividad had accumulated large amounts of gold in his absence.

Instead, he returned to find that all the men he had left behind had been killed.

Columbus had thought that the Indians were always gentle, and so was surprised to learn that they were capable of bloodshed. The natives had been provoked. They explained to Columbus that the Spaniards had wanted to keep all the native women to themselves and had claimed that they should be their mistresses. In time, the native men became jealous and killed the Spaniards. These events changed Columbus' attitude about the Indians. Soon he was sending them to Spain in shiploads where they were sold as slaves.

Columbus was a dreamer, a navigator, a businessman, and a bit of a poet. He was admired for his skills at sea, but he was otherwise not a good leader. His difficulties with his men were undoubtedly worsened because he was Genoese and a known friend of the king of Portugal. His men distrusted and disobeyed him. He made a poor Viceroy, not knowing how to run a colony. Ferdinand and Isabella gradually lost their faith in his abilities.

As time went on life became more complex and difficult for Columbus. He overstepped his authority by appointing his brother Bartholomew as governor of the newly-established colony in Santo Domingo. A group of colonists rebelled against Bartholomew. After considerable trouble, Columbus and Bartholomew were forced to allow the rebels to return to Spain. Back in Spain the rebels spread lies and negative news of the American settlement, making things difficult between Columbus and the King and Queen.

Finally, Ferdinand and Isabella decided to revoke Columbus' political authority in the New World. They sent over a new Viceroy, Francisco de Bobadilla, and empowered him to arrest any more rebels. When Columbus denied Bobadilla's authority, he was thrown in chains and shipped home to Spain to be put on trial. Aboard the ship, Columbus

"A Galway man, Patrick Maguire, was on the first voyage of Columbus and was said to be the first to set foot on American soil. He jumped from the boat and waded to land."

Frances Gibson, *The Seafarers*

"English and Irish national pride have been flattered by the idea that a man of each nation accompanied the fleet; but there was no Englishman, Irishman or other Northern European aboard."

Samuel Eliot Morison, *The Admiral of the Ocean Sea*

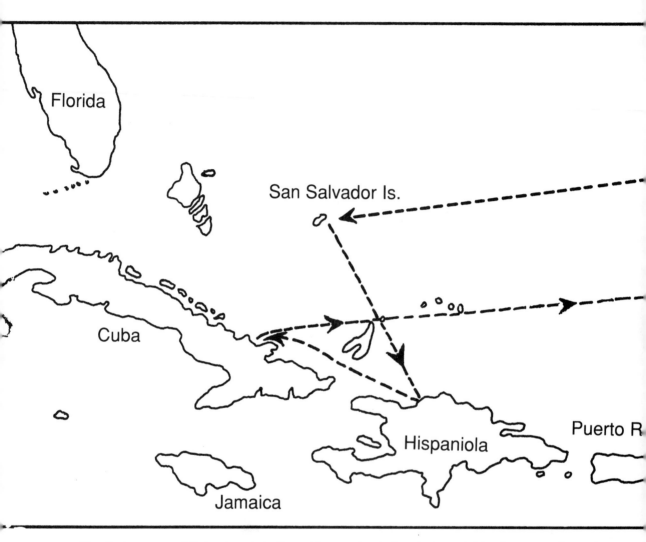

The first voyage of Columbus is believed by most scholars to have taken the route shown here. Many scholars and sailors have tried to duplicate the voyage from the ship's log that Columbus kept, but nautical terminology, wind and sea conditions, and the passage of time have made it difficult to say with certainty if these were the exact places where Columbus landed.

refused to allow the captain to remove his chains. He even wore the chains to his audience with Ferdinand and Isabella.

Though Ferdinand and Isabella refused to grant Columbus' request to revoke Bobadilla's authority, they did allow Columbus to return to the New World.

Finally, on his fourth voyage, Columbus found the gold he had been promising—in modern-day Panama. The problem, though, was mining it. The climate was hot and the Spaniards got sick. The natives were hostile and Columbus and his followers had to fight continuous battles with them.

Worse, shipworms that lived in these warmer waters attacked the hulls of the Spanish ships, quickly boring holes in their bottoms and destroying their

Columbus claimed the islands he found for his patrons, the King and Queen of Spain.

The exotic goods and stories that Columbus brought back with him to the Spanish court convinced others that the western route to the Indies would make them all wealthy.

ability to float. Columbus and his crew finally had to push their last two badly-leaking ships onto the beaches of present-day Jamaica, hundreds of miles from the nearest Europeans.

Columbus and his men were not rescued for more than a year. By then Columbus' health had taken a turn for the worse and he had only a couple of years left to live.

His final months were not particularly happy ones. His initial voyage had changed the course of European and world history forever (and he knew it), but Columbus was never given the respect and admiration he craved. Royalty and Spanish and Portuguese merchants had been enriched through his efforts, but the new lands he found were named after someone else.

Columbus believed his voyage of discovery had been God's will, and he said that God had guided him and intended only him to find the New World. He died—not in poverty, but in pain and frustration—in 1506.

Three

Did the Irish or Welsh Discover America?

In considering the discovery of America it is important that we recognize the many kinds of stories which are handed down from earlier generations and often taken for factual history.

Saint Brendan

An old legend has it that an Irish abbot known as St. Brendan "discovered" America while voyaging in the Atlantic with a boatload of monks, long before Atlantic Ocean crossings by either the Vikings or Columbus. Like so many other legends, this one undoubtedly contains at least a grain of truth. But the problem with a legend, of course, is separating the fantasy from the reality. Trying to keep fact separate from fiction is easier said than done.

We *do* know that in the Middle Ages many Irish priests and clergy were drawn to secluded places where they could establish monasteries and seek communion with God. From the Irish geographer, Dicuil, we have also learned that there were Irish monks living on the island of Iceland as early as A.D. 795.

But as it comes down to us, the Irish legend of St.

Brendan claims considerably more. According to the popular tale, St. Brendan the Navigator was originally the head of a monastery in Ireland. Over a period of three and a half years, he and his companions sailed great distances and discovered extraordinary lands. We are told they came upon islands with warm climates where it was never cold. They saw bright birds, as well as trees and plants similar to those later found in the Caribbean.

How Valid Is the Brendan Legend?

Few people doubt that there was a real Brendan. Moreover, we know the Irish were in Iceland, which suggests that their boats were not as flimsy as they look. But there are problems with the Brendan legend. For one thing, the first written record of Brendan's exploits were recorded anonymously in an eleventh-century manuscript known as *The Voyages of St. Brendan.* For 500 years people simply kept his legend alive by retelling his adventures. Indeed, so improbable are many of Brendan's doings that there is every reason to suspect that each teller tried to improve the tale by making it more incredible. The result is a yarn too fantastic for even a Hollywood movie.

Like Hollywood, the Middle Ages sometimes distinguished little between fact and fantasy, reality and hope. Times were often grim and the good things people wanted to believe were often more compelling than truth.

In those days the ability to write was largely limited to priests and monks. As representatives of the church, they believed it was essential to turn people's minds away from pre-Christian myths and fantastic tales and toward Christian views. Not surprisingly, then, Brendan is made constantly to sermonize and pray in ways that seem calculated to inspire Christians. His most fantastic adventures are clearly intended as "spiritual" lessons.

Early sailors constructed small boats of many styles and using many different materials. The coracles of the Irish were made from wood and animal skins; this boat from Egypt was made from bundles of papyrus. In both cases, the size of the crafts was limited by the material. Could a voyage of thousands of miles be made in such boats?

For instance, on arriving at a particularly beautiful and idyllic island, Brendan and his followers met humanlike creatures with the heads of pigs. They learned that these creatures were fallen angels who, because of the sin of pride, were destined never to see God. On the last leg of the voyage, Brendan was trapped by a giant fish for forty days. Finally, after returning home to Ireland, Brendan ascended bodily into heaven. Obviously, Brendan's fantastic adventures could not have happened quite as they were eventually reported.

There are also reasons to doubt that Brendan sailed as far as has been claimed. *Coracles*, as their boats were called, had skeletons of wood and were covered with greased and waterproofed animal skins. They were low, and, if well-handled, could survive a storm, but they had primitive steering devices and were extremely difficult to navigate. Larger coracles had small square sails but smaller coracles were powered only by oars. These were not meant for long ocean voyages.

The Brendan Influence

The Brendan legend, however, is not without value to early American history. And there are a couple of surprising reasons why Brendan's story is important.

When it finally reached manuscript form, Brendan's tale became a kind of medieval bestseller. It was translated into French, Norwegian, Flemish, Spanish, German, and Italian. Since we know from his early biographers that Columbus was a passionate reader of any stories about exploration and adventure, there is good reason to suppose he read about the Irish abbot's adventures and found in them a source of inspiration for his own.

In fact, Brendan's voyages inspired many European navigators and explorers — especially the Portuguese. While Columbus was growing up,

Prince Henry the Navigator, ruler of Portugal in the fifteenth century, sent his sea captains to find the mythical islands of St. Brendan. They discovered the Azores off the coast of Africa instead, and claimed them for Portugal.

Portugal was ruled by a king called Prince Henry the Navigator. Henry's captains sailed west in search of the mythical St. Brendan's Isles. In so doing, they discovered the Azores, a chain of islands. The furthest of these islands are nearly a thousand miles off the western shores of Portugal. The last of them were not discovered until after the birth of Columbus. Columbus used these islands as a supply base and an outpost during the course of his four trips to the New World.

Another adventurer of the time was a man named Pedro Vasques de Frontera. In service to Prince Henry, in 1452, Vasques accompanied Diogo de Tieve, the discoverer of Flores and Corvo, the Azores furthest from Portugal. Daringly, Diogo and Vasques headed due north from these last discoveries, traveling to the latitude of Ireland before returning to Portugal. Afterwards, Vasques was certain that they had been near land before deciding to return to Europe.

As it happened, shortly before Columbus embarked on his historic voyage, Vasques met him. He encouraged Columbus to believe there was land west of the Azores. But perhaps more importantly, he lent his reputation to the Columbian enterprise, encouraging young men to volunteer and sail with the newly-appointed Admiral.

Madoc

According to a twelfth-century legend, a Welsh prince named Madoc became frustrated that his many brothers were fighting over who would inherit the wealth of their dead father. He gathered a few men and sailed far into the west. After a long voyage, he discovered a fruitful and pleasant land. On returning to Wales, he recruited a large group of people and left once again to establish a settlement in these new lands. Since Madoc and his compatriots never returned to Wales, it was widely supposed that his new settlement was successful.

In the early seventeenth century, Spain took an interest in the rumors about Madoc and alerted Spanish explorers to be on the lookout for white Indians—Native Americans who might look as though they had inherited European blood.

The Madoc legend was almost 600 years old by the time Spain decided to investigate it. And of course the Madoc story, like that of Brendan, was 500 years old before it was ever written down. Madoc's tale first appeared in Dr. Richard Powell's 1584 *History of Cambria*, a work written nearly 100 years after Columbus' historic voyage.

Some believe the Madoc tale was made up after the Columbus discovery in an attempt to justify English involvement in the New World. But even if it was not, it was still hundreds of years old before it was ever written down. That being so, we are left to wonder—what did the Madoc story lose or gain during the centuries of its retelling?

The Madoc story differs considerably from Brendan's. With Madoc, there are no tales of sea monsters, fallen angels, or religious experiences—he simply disappears. Madoc voyaged into the west and left to unborn generations of Welsh and English

Madoc sails from Wales, circa A.D. 1170.

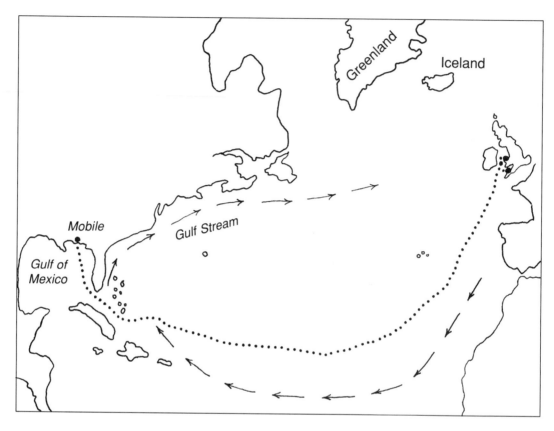

One version of how Madoc may have travelled to the New World.

storytellers the question of what happened to him.

Thanks to an existing Native American legend, the Madoc story has been made to seem more believable. Many natives of Central America or *Mesoamerica* claimed that they were descended from white men who had come to Mexico out of the rising sun. The Madoc legend inspired the belief that Madoc and his companions had settled down among the Indians. This made a certain kind of sense in a region where the natives were often lighter-skinned than elsewhere, and where their mode of dress seemed to resemble that of the Welsh of the twelfth century.

There are also other traditions and beliefs about the mysterious Madoc. In his sixteenth-century exploration of the present-day southern United States, Hernando DeSoto reported finding the remains of ancient fortifications at the mouth of Mobile Bay, Alabama. He did not think the Indians were capable of building them. The local chapter of the Daughters of the American Revolution took his claim seriously enough that they erected a memorial plaque at Fort Morgan, in 1953. It reads: "In memory of Prince Madoc, a Welsh explorer, who landed on the shores of Mobile bay in 1170 and left behind, with the Indians, the Welsh Language."

The Daughters of the American Revolution believed the language of the Welsh as spoken in the twelfth century was similar to the language of the Mandan Indians who originally lived in the area. Amateur linguists living in America in the nineteenth century claimed that they had discovered similar sounds in Welsh and the Mandan language. On the basis of certain word similarities, they concluded that the Mandan tribe had once welcomed Madoc and his followers. Some people also claimed that the Welsh and the Mandans even produced an occasional blue-eyed, blond Indian. Thus the Madoc story became an enduring European fantasy about American natives.

While there were occasional reports of blue-eyed Indians, no sizable group of European settlers ever recorded seeing these supposed "Euro-Indians." In fact, every sighting of a blue-eyed Indian seems to have been an isolated episode. One person might report seeing such people, but others living in the same area at the same time never made similar sightings of their own.

Geoffrey Ashe, a scholar inclined to accept that Brendan may have voyaged to the New World, is more skeptical about Madoc. He points out that the Indians supposedly connected with Madoc are always said to be beyond the most recent zone of European settlement. That is, European newcomers

"The inscriptions are written in various European and Mediterranean languages in alphabets that date from 2,500 years ago, and they speak not only of visits by ancient ships, but also of permanent colonies of Celts, Basques, Libyans, and even Egyptians. They occur on buried temples, on tablets and on gravestones and on cliff faces. From some of them we infer that the colonists intermarried with the Amerindians, and so their descendants still live here today."

Barry Fell, *America B.C.*

"Chance crevices in rocks, Indian petroglyphs, schoolboy pranks, outright hoaxes were all being 'interpreted' by enthusiasts with no training in linguistics but who wished to people America's past with Viking hordes. ....A truly impressive number of citizens will rally around any asserted exploit, however disprovable, by early Vikings."

Erik Wahlgren, *The Vikings and America*

Prom Lupi.

The "discovery" of the different tribal peoples in America was made piecemeal by French, Spanish, English and Dutch explorers. This engraving depicts the arrival of the Huguenots (French Protestants) in Florida.

could never confirm any sighting. In every instance, the Indians had reportedly moved on. Finally, of course, with America overrun with European settlers, there was no place for them to have moved to, and still no blue-eyed Indians ever appeared. "So expired, for practical purposes," wrote Ashe, "a claim which was almost certainly nothing but... invention."

From a nautical standpoint it is possible that Madoc could have voyaged to the New World. Because of extended contacts between the Norse and the Welsh before and during Madoc's time, Madoc certainly would have had access to Viking ship-building skills. Though there is no written evidence, it is even possible that before his own voyage Madoc had journeyed to Iceland and heard Viking explorers talk of an abundant land to the west—a place they called Vinland.

However, even if Madoc did sail across the Atlantic and find a new land there, he would have arrived in the New World a century after the Vikings.

Four

Who Were the Bold Men From the North?

"For nearly 350 years we and our fathers have lived in this lovely land, and never before has such a terror appeared in Britain as we have now suffered from a pagan people, nor was it thought that such an attack from the sea was possible. Behold the church of St. Cuthbert spattered with the blood of the priests of God, despoiled of all its ornaments. A place more venerable than any in Britain has become prey to pagan peoples."

So wrote a monk named Alcuin after a Viking raiding party destroyed the monastery where he lived at Lindisfarne off the Northumbrian coast of England in about A.D. 793.

Indeed, for the next three hundred years, the plundering Vikings (or Norsemen) would strike fear in the hearts of virtually anyone in Europe living near a large body of water. Ireland, Wales, Scotland, England, France, the Netherlands, Germany—all of these countries bled and learned to fear the wide-bladed Norse sword and broadaxe.

The people we call Vikings came from Scandinavian lands—Denmark and Sweden, but primarily

The Vikings were the dominant sea-going people of Northern Europe,
feared by any country with shores to defend.

Norway. These are northern European countries whose dark, wet, and cold climate is isolating. Yet the navigable waters that surround these lands have long provided avenues to the warmer, sometimes more developed lands to the south. The Vikings learned to build ships which would sail "the sea roads." And they developed the skills of war that allowed them to take advantage of the disorganized condition of Europe before A.D. 1000.

Hardy, restless, and violent, the Vikings were among the world's first guerilla warriors. They came out of nowhere to prey on villages and small towns along the many seacoasts of Europe, even ranging into the Mediterranean. They took whatever they wanted, showed their enemies no mercy, and quickly departed before any larger group could be brought against them. Along with seaworthy ships, they had the courage and endurance to dare turbulent seas that others would not.

They were not a literate culture, but they valued family loyalty, a good memory, bravery in battle, and forthrightness in speech. They committed to memory family histories and other important events and recited them on special occasions. This way of passing on history is called the oral tradition. The *Icelandic Sagas*, for example, survived as a part of this oral tradition for many years before being written down.

What Are the *Icelandic Sagas*?

The *Icelandic Sagas* are a cycle of old Norse stories which chronicle the adventures of various Viking seafarers. The *Sagas* that concern historians of early America are few and are contained in several old manuscripts largely concerned with the Erickson clan. None were written down until well after the events in question happened.

Nevertheless, historians regard these tales as significant in many respects. One of the most important

The *Icelandic Sagas* began as tales told by bards (storytellers who sang) describing the great voyages and battles of the Vikings.

54

"Six Icelandic annals record that in 1121 Eric, bishop of Greenland, sailed to Vinland. At the beginning of the twelfth century there would appear to have been a Christian colony in Vinland."

Frances Gibson, *The Seafarers*

"The time span of the entire Vinland story in the two sagas probably centers on the year 1000, the possibility being that Leif found Vinland in the 990s, and that Karlsefni may have given up on the new lands by 1012 at the latest. No greater degree of chronological precision is currently possible."

Erik Wahlgren, *The Vikings in America*

things about them is that we know they were all written down many years before Columbus set sail on his historic voyage. This means that however we evaluate what they say, they do provide us with reliable evidence that new lands west of Iceland and Greenland were known and talked about by some people before Columbus.

The *Icelandic Sagas* manuscripts differ somewhat from one another, since each storyteller probably heard and repeated his tale a bit differently. But generally, those who have closely studied the *Sagas* are impressed with how little they vary. Scholars feel that the resemblances from saga to saga show that the Vikings valued accuracy more highly than literary flair. This makes them more reliable as historical records than the legends we have already discussed.

Even so, for a long time tales of Norse expeditions to the New World were taken seriously only by a handful of Scandinavian scholars. It wasn't until archaeologists found that the Vikings had lived three or four hundred years in Greenland that opinions began to change. Given the well-known Viking restlessness, it seemed more likely that Vikings had reached North America during those long years in Greenland.

While still pagan, the restless Vikings loved to raid European seacoasts and plunder churches. But the Vikings loved battle too well and often fought among themselves. Often at issue were small kingdoms and armies. Until about the middle of the ninth century, warrior king fought warrior king. Then things began to change.

About the middle of the ninth century, a certain Viking chief known as Harold Fairhair decided to make himself king of all Norway. Fairhair proved successful, and his disorganized enemies were obliged to leave the country.

A man named Ingold, probably an enemy of Fairhair, voyaged west from Norway and settled in

The Vikings reached Greenland before A.D. 1000.

Iceland about A.D. 870. Despite the island's formidable name, the climate of Iceland is rather mild. Before long, other Norse immigrants began arriving. Within a short time, Iceland had a population of nearly fifty thousand people. A few of these immigrants would become legendary names in an intriguing bit of history.

What the *Icelandic Sagas* Tell Us

The *Icelandic Sagas* introduce us to life in Iceland about A.D. 982, when a farmer-chief named Erik the Red got into trouble for killing a man named Valthjof.

Erik and his father had already been banished from Norway to Iceland for murder. Now, with the murder of Valthjof, Erik was expelled from Iceland for three years. Having nowhere else to go, Erik decided to voyage west in search of lands that he had heard lay beyond Iceland.

The land he found was harsh, barren, and rocky—anything but green. But Vikings took hardship in stride, and after three years, Erik sailed home to Iceland in search of others to help him settle permanently in the new land. Cleverly, Erik decided to name the new land Greenland, arguing that settlers would be attracted to the place if it had a good name.

Erik soon set sail again for Greenland with a small fleet. Aboard his twenty-five ships were women, livestock, and those supplies necessary to create a permanent settlement. Because of storms and icebergs, only fourteen ships made it. But more ships arrived later, and other settlements followed.

Shortly after Erik's party arrived, another man named Bjarni Herjolfsson decided to sail to Greenland to join his father. Bjarni's ship, blown off course by a severe storm, was forced south and west of Greenland. Eventually, he sighted land. But when he saw that the land was not mountainous (as he knew Greenland to be), he realized he had probably gone too far. His men, intrigued by this interesting-looking land, begged him to put ashore and explore it. But Bjarni refused. Instead, he retraced his course, sailing back north and east until he saw the land he knew must be Greenland.

Erik's Sons Continue the Exploration

The story of Bjarni's accidental voyage to the strange land persisted in Greenland, however. A few years later, Erik's son Leif decided to go in search of it. He bought Bjarni's ship and gathered a crew of thirty-five men. His father declined to accompany him, giving his advanced age as an excuse, so Leif set sail without him.

According to the *Sagas*, the first land they saw was primarily flat rock with glaciers in the background. Leif named this *Helluland* ("the land of flat stone"). Setting sail to the south, they came on yet another land, this one low-lying and timbered. They called it *Markland* (or "timbered land"). They sailed on yet farther and found a third land where a river came out of a lake. They sailed up the river and saw that the land was very pleasant. There was no end of salmon in the water and the grass grew all year and would have been ideal fodder for livestock. They decided to stay for a time. Unloading their ship, they set about building houses.

One evening a man named Tyker got lost while on an exploring mission. When a search party finally found him, Tyker reported that he had found grapes similar to those that grew in his homeland. Thereafter, Leif began to call this new land *Vinland*, or "Wineland."

Leif finally returned to Greenland after wintering in Vinland. Leif's brother Thorvald, however, felt that Leif had not explored thoroughly enough. So Thorvald borrowed Leif's ship and set sail for Vinland himself.

Arriving at Leif's old campsite, Thorvald and his

"The Beardmore finds…seem well established, and so do the fourteenth-century Kensington rune inscription in Minnesota and a dozen Norse artifacts…in the form of halberds, axes, spearheads, fire steels, and so forth dug up within a hundred miles or so of Kensington."

Frederick J. Pohl, *The Lost Discovery*

"The objects would appear to be genuine Norse antiquities. Whether or not they were taken to America in the early middle ages, however, is an altogether different matter. The balance of probability, indeed, is that they were brought there, not in the Viking era, but in comparatively recent times, by one Lieutenant John Block, a Norwegian."

C.J. Marcus, *The Conquest of the North Atlantic*

The wounding of Thorvald. The "Skraelings" of the *Vinland Sagas* (part of the *Icelandic Sagas*) probably refers to the Native American Indian tribes.

crew wintered there. In the spring they went exploring. Thorvald and his men spent the better part of two years exploring by land and sea. Then Thorvald was killed in an attack by men the Vikings called *Skraelings*—undoubtedly the same people our ancestors would call Indians. After burying Thorvald in Vinland, his men returned to Greenland.

Another brother, Thorstein, wanted to recover Thorvald's body. He set sail for Vinland with his wife, Gudrid, and twenty-five men. Shortly after arriving, however, Thorstein was stricken with the plague and died. Gudrid returned to Greenland, where she met and married a man named Thorfinn Karlsefni.

An Attempt to Colonize

At her urging, Karlsefni took a large group to Vinland. At first all went well. Once there they settled in and began trading with the Skraelings who lived near their settlement. If the tales are correct, Gudrid then gave birth to a boy named Snorri, who became the first European to be born in the New World.

But trouble began again. When a new tribe of Skraelings moved into the area near the settlement, the Vikings were attacked. Following a particularly fierce battle, Karlsefni was determined to return to Greenland. Though there may have been one or two other attempts to colonize Vinland after that, and though the Greenland Vikings almost certainly sent periodic wood-gathering expeditions to Vinland in years to come, the *Sagas* end here.

For a long time the *Sagas* gathered dust in remote places. They seemed mysterious—particularly to a world that had already decided that Columbus had discovered America. Yet those who studied the *Sagas* found them hard to forget. They seemed, at the very least, honest tales concerned with men and women of great strength and courage.

"There has been some disagreement among scholars as to the location of Vinland. However, this disagreement is now largely a thing of the past, and most writers on the Norse discovery of America are agreed that Vinland was somewhere in the south coast of New England."

Hjalmar Holand, *America 1355 To 1364*

"Tornoe argues that there were such settlements between Nova Scotia and Chesapeake Bay and concludes that there was one on Manhattan Island, Gathorne-Hardy is among the conservative scholars who think the Norse never pushed further south than eastern Canada, while Reman argues for landings in the Hudson Bay area. Enterline speculates with utter sincerity that an important area of Norse interest was Alaska."

Eugene R. Fingerhut, *Who First Discovered America? A Critique of Pre-Columbian Voyages*

Thorfinn and Gudrid in Vinland.

As men studied the geography of the north, the proximity of Greenland to northern Canada, and the length of time that the Vikings had lived in Greenland, the claims of the *Sagas* began to seem more reasonable.

During the nineteenth century, people who studied early Norse history began to state their belief that it was likely that the Norse had been to America before Columbus.

Claiming something probably happened was not enough, of course. Where was the proof? After all, if the *Sagas* claimed there had been at least three different visits, should not the Vikings have left some sign of themselves? Where—if they had been here—was the evidence of their presence in the New World?

Five

Does the Evidence Support the Icelandic Sagas?

In the nineteenth century industrialization was in full swing. Both Europe and America became sentimental about the past. Stories about Vikings became very popular, and experts and amateurs alike wrote books about them. None of these books, however, could expect to be very popular without a stand on the Vinland question. Were the Vikings in America before Columbus or not?

In book after book, the debate continued. Those who were skeptical said that if the Vikings had been here they would have left some trace. So they demanded proof—physical evidence. In response, many writers encouraged readers to be on the lookout for "finds" that would finally show that the Vikings had indeed been in America.

The Unearthing of the Kensington Stone

In 1898 a Swedish immigrant named Olof Ohman uprooted a tree on his farm near Kensington, Minnesota, and found a strange stone tangled up in its roots. It was a slab, roughly rectangular, like a tombstone. It was about two and a half feet high, between two and three inches thick, fifteen inches wide, and

Opposite page: the expeditions of Erik the Red and his son, Leif, may have explored all of these areas in North America.

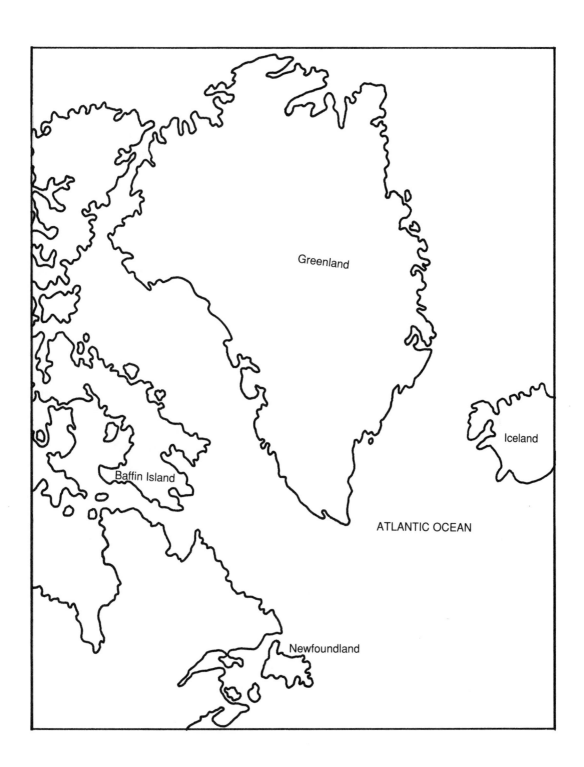

weighed approximately two hundred pounds.

According to what Ohman later told authorities, his ten-year-old son Edward was with him when he saw the stone. The boy apparently poked the slab with a stick and noticed characters carved in the rock face. When all the dirt and grime had been removed, the carved symbols were recognized as runes.

Runes are simple characters that were used in early writing in German and Scandinavian countries. Since northern European cultures lacked paper and pens, writers often carved short messages in rocks and wood. Ancient runestones had been found all over northern Europe. But until Ohman's, no runestone had captured the popular imagination in America.

Soon Ohman's stone was seen by many of his Scandinavian neighbors. Some of them had books about runic characters and made efforts to translate the writing on the Kensington Stone. Excitement in Minnesota and throughout America ran very high. The following is a widely accepted translation made in 1958 by Erik Wahlgren, formerly a professor of Scandinavian languages at the University of California. Wahlgren spent many years studying this stone.

8 Swedes and 22 Norwegians on an exploration journey from Vinland westward. We had our camp by 2 rocky islets one day's journey north of this stone. We were out fishing one day. When we came home we found 10 men red with blood and dead. AVM save us from evil. We have 10 men by the sea to look after our ships, 14 days' journey from this island. Year 1362.

To Scandinavian-Americans here was proof at last. The translated runes seemed to indicate that the *Icelandic Sagas* were accurate, that Norsemen had landed in North America long before the arrival of Columbus.

The Kensington Stone, found on a farm in rural Minnesota, was the subject of much debate because of the mysterious runes carved upon it.

"All the objections that have been raised by the inscription's opponents have been shown to be invalid. On the proponents' side the "clinchers" are, it seems to me, three: 1) the presence of archaisms in the language… which no likely forger could have known; 2) the weathering of the incisions; and 3) the stone's having been found in a sealed stratum."

Robert A. Hall, "The Kensington Stone is Genuine," 1982

"1) The Kensington Stone was found in a Scandinavian immigrant community. 2) The style, spelling, grammar, numerals, and contents of the inscription on the stone forbid our thinking it medieval; but they are supremely appropriate to a writing in Minnesota dialect. 3) No reliable evidence has been adduced for believing in the stone, thus inscribed, to have been extracted from the roots of a tree."

Erik Wahlgren, *The Kensington Stone*

Many, however, found the stone very odd. The *Icelandic Sagas* end shortly after the year A.D. 1000. They did not claim that Viking explorers had journeyed far inland. Yet here was evidence that Vikings had traveled as far south and west as Minnesota three hundred years after the Sagas ended. Had North America been continuously occupied ever since the Vikings' arrival about A.D. 1000? What did the stone mean about their ships being a fourteen-day journey from the "island?" The stone was found on a farm, not an island. How could a ship be only fourteen days away from this spot in western Minnesota when in those days there was no ocean access to the Great Lakes?

Skeptics questioned the stone's legitimacy. They pointed out that many magazines and newspapers had been publishing speculative stories and articles about the Viking presence in America. It seemed too much of a coincidence, they argued, that such a stone should be found and made public by those who had only recently come to America from Scandinavian countries.

Though the stone was publicized in newspapers and magazines, and though many people wanted the stone's message to be true, experts who had studied medieval Scandinavian languages and runic characters said it was a fake.

It was a fact, experts explained, that people living in one region used different runes to write the same message. And just as the English spoken in the American classroom today differs from the English spoken by Shakespeare, so the Swedish, Norwegian, and Danish languages have been spoken differently at different times in history. Therefore, rune scholars say they can judge with a high degree of accuracy the historical time period and region in which the runestone was carved and the language of any rune carver.

While most people could learn to copy a few

runes from a book and create some sort of message on a stone, amateurs attempting to carve such a message would find it difficult to fool runologists—people who are experts in runes.

After a great deal of early publicity and many expressions of popular support, the Kensington Stone was sent to two important authorities in the Midwest. Linguist and runologist Olaus J. Breda stated in no uncertain terms that it was a fake. George O. Curme, a professor of history at Northwestern University, agreed.

In their view, the stone mixed runes from different regions and different times. It used words and phrases not seen in the fourteenth century—expressions they said very much resembled the slang used by nineteenth-century Scandinavian farmers living in the Midwest. They said the writer of the stone had not known how to write numbers in runes. Finally, they argued that the characters appeared to be recently carved.

The Kensington Stone was returned to Ohman. He did not admit that the stone was a hoax. But neither did he argue for its legitimacy. In fact, he used it as a stepladder to his granary. Others were not willing to give up the struggle to have the Kensington Stone accepted, however.

Despite the verdict of scholars, many people continued to insist the stone was real and mounted clever arguments in its defense. They said that the stone's incredible message—hard to believe though it was—was actually an argument for its validity. Anybody serious about fooling people would have tried to create a less sensational message, they argued. They proposed that perhaps much of Ohman's farm had been underwater at the time the stone was carved. After all, Minnesota was known as the land of a thousand lakes. If so, then the hill where the stone was found might once have been a small island. Perhaps in slightly warmer times there had been a

Viking handiwork: the wooden stem-post from a Viking ship, fashioned like a dragon head.

water route from the Great Lakes to the Atlantic Ocean. Believers argued that if the stonecarver was attempting to fool people, he would have dated it closer to Leif Erickson's time, about 1008, rather than 1362.

Though Ohman, whose English was reportedly weak, never did try to prove the authenticity of the stone he had unearthed, another Scandinavian immigrant took up that mission.

The Role of Hjalmar Rued Holand

Hjalmar Rued Holand, a Norwegian who had immigrated to the United States, first took an interest in the stone around 1907—after it had already been pronounced a fake by Breda and Curme. Holand had worked as a fruit farmer, furniture salesman, and real estate agent. He had also written about the

Norwegian settlements in the United States. He was not a trained scholar and knew little of archaeology, runes, or the study of languages, but he very much believed the stone was authentic.

Holand acquired the stone from Ohman and had it shipped to his own home in Wisconsin. Holand was to spend the rest of his life writing, speaking about, and defending the authenticity of the Kensington Stone.

In 1910, Professor George T. Flom, a linguist from the University of Illinois, a man who had personally examined the stone, said that the inscription was "modern," and that it was clear to him that the stone had been "planted, later to be discovered." That same year, another group of seven scholars

The hilt of this Viking sword is decorated with silver and gold.

from the University of Illinois reached a similar conclusion about the falseness of the stone. In each instance scholars tended to reject the Kensington Stone on the same grounds. In part, they concluded:

1. The stone carver had confused runes used in one geographic region with runes in use in another.

2. The stone carver had mixed styles of early runes with those not used until later.

3. The stone carver had used a method of numbering that was not employed until many years after its fourteenth-century date.

4. The stone carver had used runes in ways that suggested he was unfamiliar with simple rules of writing employed in the fourteenth century.

5. The stone carver had used slang more in keeping with nineteenth-century Scandinavian farmers than with fourteenth-century Vikings.

6. The runes appeared to have been recently carved or at least were not at all weathered.

7. The stone was found in a Scandinavian community where many people were already very familiar with the Vikings-versus-Columbus debate.

8. Ohman never made any effort to defend the authenticity of the stone.

Nevertheless, these objections did not stop Holand. Instead they seemed to fuel his enthusiasm for proving the stone had been carved by Vikings. Many Americans wanted to believe Holand's increasingly fanciful theories about the stone, so they continued to contact him whenever they believed they had found new evidence of Vikings in America.

In search of support for his theories, Holand took the stone to Europe, where, unfortunately for him, French and Norwegian scholars also declined to accept the stone as genuine.

One of the stone's most emphatic critics was Erik Moltke of Denmark's National Museum. Moltke wrote of the inscription that it was "suspect in every detail, in rune forms, grammar, syntax, vocabulary, in the weathering of the runes, in the history of the find... Never," he concluded, "has a spurious document stood on such feeble ground and given such striking proofs of its falsity."

The stone's finder, Olof Ohman, never confessed that the Kensington Stone had been a hoax, but on his deathbed one of Ohman's friends told his grown children that he had been active in carving the runes. After having once supported the stone as a Viking artifact, the Minnesota Historical Society eventually issued a report saying that the stone was not genuine.

Despite the addition of a second taped confession offered by another friend of Ohman who had been a party to the hoax, despite the stone's disavowal by the Minnesota Historical Society, and despite the stone's failure to win the acceptance of authorities, there are still those who continue to accept the stone as genuine. It is enshrined at the Runestone Museum in Alexandria, Minnesota. In 1964, the Kensington Stone was sent to New York to be a part of the World's Fair. And a replica of the stone is on exhibit in the National Museum in Washington, D.C.

Though one promising bit of evidence for the Viking discovery of America seemed to be false, there were other possibilities to consider.

The Newport Tower

Convinced that the Kensington Stone was a Viking artifact, Hjalmar Rued Holand spent more than 50 years looking for evidence that would connect the stone to other found objects and prove what he believed to be true—that the Vikings had explored America in the fourteenth century. Holand turned his attention to an obscure tower in Newport, Rhode Island.

This three-story stone tower had long been a mystery to people living in the area. No one, it seemed, knew when it had been built. With no written infor-

The Old Stone Mill in Newport, Rhode Island, sometimes called the "Newport Tower." Did the Vikings build this tower hundreds of years before Columbus?

mation available, people began accepting the conclusions of a handful of amateur historians and romantics and called it the Viking Tower. No less an American poet than Henry Wadsworth Longfellow used the tower in a famous love poem called "The Skeleton in Armor."

Working from the idea that no one knew when the tower had been built, Holand published in 1946 a detailed book about what he supposed were the origins of the tower, its purposes, its occupants, and history. In *America 1355-1364*, Holand speculated the tower had been built by Vikings so that they could look out to sea and keep watch for their companions. He told his readers that some Vikings stayed in Rhode Island while their companions went exploring. Other explorers in the party, Holand claimed, voyaged to Minnesota, ran into trouble, and there carved the Kensington Stone.

Unfortunately, Holand's argument did not hold up. In all that was written about the first white settlement built in Newport, Rhode Island, in 1649, there was not a single mention of the dramatic tower. Had the tower already existed in 1649 when colonists came to the area, a great deal would have been written about it. Everyone would have been asking how it could have come to be in such a place.

As it happened, the Tower was first mentioned in the 1677 will of Governor Benedict Arnold, where it was described as "my stone wind-miln." Because popular emotion was running so high in favor of accepting the Viking origins of the tower, scientists made a careful study of it in 1948-49. They even dug beneath its foundations. Among the objects they found there were the stems of pipes used by American colonists for smoking tobacco. They also found other articles that could be dated to about the year 1750.

The Vinland Map

Holand died in 1963. If he had lived longer he

"In October, 1941, I made my first inspection of the Newport Tower. Most of its details were familiar to me through reading, but a personal inspection is necessary to comprehend the significance of the many details, and to sense fully the ancient atmosphere of this stone ruin, so unlike any structure of today, or even of the Colonial period of New England. It is a priceless heirloom, the only building in America that brings us in contact with the Middle Ages."

Hjalmar Holand, *America 1355-1364*

"The earliest finds associated with the building were no older than the seventeenth century....Sparse as they were, the finds were conclusive, for they consisted of fragments of clay pipe, datable pottery, glass, a gun flint, and nails—together with chips and pieces of mortar...[they] point to a date of building well within the seventeenth century."

Birgitta Wallace, "Some Points of Controversy"

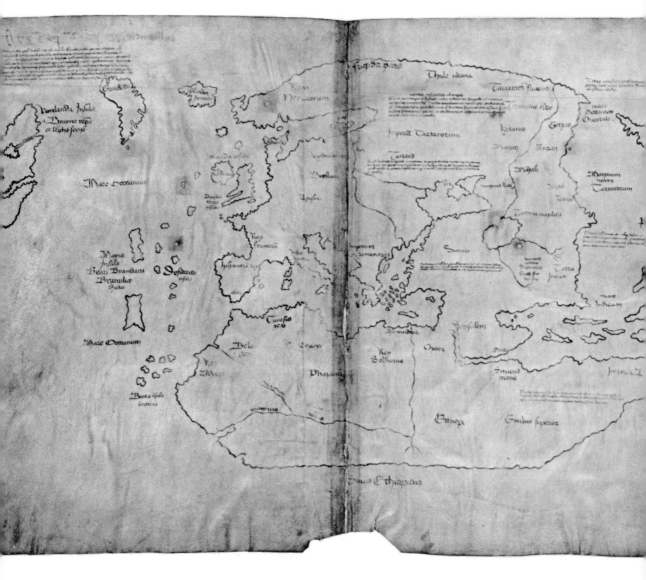

The "Vinland Map" excited scholars who believed it proved that Vikings knew about North America long before Columbus and his fellow explorers from the fifteenth and sixteenth centuries.

would probably have become involved in the next famous Viking find that appeared on the scene a couple of years after his death.

The world of historians was rocked on Columbus Day, 1965, when a man named Raleigh A. Skelton announced the publication of a map of Vinland—supposedly drawn in 1440—fifty-two years before the Columbus voyage.

If genuine, the implications of the Vinland Map were inescapable. It meant that men had known about the New World more than fifty years before Columbus had set sail. It also meant that the coast of North America had been well-explored and that Greenland was known by men of those times to be an island.

The story of how the map was discovered is revealing. It demonstrates the problems experienced by scholars searching for an accurate understanding of the past.

One day in 1957 an American bookdealer named Laurence Witten went to the Yale University Library. Witten showed a man named Thomas E. Marston a very interesting old manuscript. As the Library's Curator of Medieval and Renaissance Literature collection and an expert in old books, Marston was quite excited by what he saw. He asked Witten for time to make a careful examination of it.

Witten gave Marston the small volume. It contained the Vinland map and twenty-one pages of text from a work called *The Tartar Relation*, the story of a thirteenth-century monk's journey to Asia. Because other copies of the story were available, Marston did not consider the text particularly valuable. He was, however, very excited by the map.

Marston consulted R.A. Skelton and George D. Painter, two experts in medieval writing and maps with the British Museum in England.

Over a period of several years, Skelton and Painter subjected the map and manuscripts to extensive testing. They concluded that the 1440 dating of the map fit the style of handwriting on the map. They traced the parchment and the paper to a mill in Switzerland that was in operation in 1453, and generally found the map to be what it claimed.

Marston, Skelton, and Raleigh collaborated on a book about the important discovery of the map. The book contained a reproduction of the map and a discussion of the many tests they had done on it as well as the many questions that it raised about medieval geography. The book sold a great many copies. Yet things were not as they seemed.

Scholars Question the Map's Authenticity

After an initially favorable reaction, scholars began to suspect that the map might be a fraud. They observed that it was drawn in a different style from other maps made in that area at that particular time. It had been drawn without a border, with no attempt at scale, no directional indicators, and no date or author listed. Most medieval maps included those things.

Besides several unlikely misspellings, the map showed a lack of knowledge about how to translate Norse family names into Latin (the language in which the map was written). Also, the map had been washed to "clean" it, an action that added to its aged appearance.

Finally, the map mentioned an 1117 voyage supposedly undertaken from Greenland to Vinland by a bishop named Henricus. It seemed strange that of many things that might have been said about the land of Vinland or Greenland, the mapmaker only mentioned the discoverers (Bjarni and Leif) and the voyage of the bishop. Nothing was said of the geography of the lands themselves. The map did not mention the Skraelings, nor the locations of the Viking settlements. Neither did it mention, as most maps of the time did, landmarks, plants, and animals.

Eventually, the trail of the bishop Henricus led to the map's discrediting. Only one other scholar had ever mentioned Henricus—a man named Luka Jelic. Like the mapmaker, Jelic never said where he got his information about Henricus. Unfortunately, Jelic died in 1924, long before anybody could ask him about his sources of information.

A closer look into Jelic's background and his scholarship made investigators believe that he had concocted the story about Henricus' voyage to Vinland in order to bolster both his own career and the flagging prestige of the Christian church in Europe.

It appears that Jelic had written about a false bishop named Henricus who was sent to Vinland. He then reinforced his claims about Henricus by drawing a false map of Vinland, mentioning Henricus in the map's legend, and then inserting the map into a book of very old manuscripts. As a church scholar he would have had access to many old manuscripts. The theory was that he had hidden this particular manuscript, but not so well that it would never be found.

The map seemed conclusively discredited in 1974 when a test done on its ink revealed it contained a modern chemical called anatase, which was not used in ink until the 1920s. Although some people have downplayed the significance of this chemical analysis, the other arguments are impossible to resist. In fact, Yale University (the publisher) has since declared that the Vinland Map is a clever forgery.

Despite the many sensational fakes associated with pre-Columbian America scholarship, most authorities did not despair when the Vinland Map was added to the long list of false evidence. Aware of how long the Vikings had been in Greenland, many scholars continued to believe that it was only a matter of time before something new would prove the Vikings had been here prior to Columbus. They

"The Vinland Map…contains Latin legends which state that Henricus, the Icelander Erik Gnupsson, sailed to Vinland and stayed there 'a long time, summer and winter.' Henricus was 'special legate from Pope Paschal' to Greenland and Vinland, a position he held from 1112 to 1122."

Frances Gibson, *The Seafarers*

"Suspicions of forgery, so far from being dispelled, progressively increased and intensified; and in the face of the very formidable body of criticism…'the most tremendous historical discovery of the twentieth century' finally toppled down like a house of cards."

C.J. Marcus, *The Conquest of the North Atlantic*

had many reasons for this.

First, the thousand years separating twentieth-century America from the Vikings is not a long time to archaeologists. Enough is known about the Vikings to enable us to read their runes, recognize their handicrafts and arts, and perhaps most importantly, to read the written records their contemporaries left behind in Norway, Iceland, and Greenland.

Second, the *Icelandic Sagas* about voyages to Greenland and Vinland were in manuscript form before the 1492 voyage (unlike other manuscripts that claimed the Irish or Welsh had been to America first). Also, unlike the various Irish and Welsh legends which make their heroes larger than life, the Sagas occasionally say unflattering things about the Viking explorers. The Sagas are about important events, not heroic men. This implies an interest in history as it happened.

Third, we know that the Vikings lived in Greenland for four hundred years. Since they were daring sailors, and since the distance from Greenland to Canada's Baffin Island is only about 300 miles, it seems reasonable that Vikings would in time reach the near parts of North America.

Fourth, the Vikings had seaworthy ships. By and large the Irish coracles and the boats of other peoples seem inadequate to the stormy seas between northern Europe and North America.

Lastly, there are the findings of Helge Ingstad.

Discovery In Newfoundland

In the 1950s, a Norwegian archaeologist named Helge Ingstad was exploring Norse ruins in Greenland. It suddenly occurred to him that the word *Vinland*, which had always been translated as "a region of grapes," could in another, rarer usage be translated as "land of meadows."

With that in mind, and with the help of boats and airplanes, he began scouting the coastline of

A Viking ceremonial axe head, probably from the tenth century A.D.

Newfoundland in Canada. It was, after all, a region with many meadows, and a land whose shores lay relatively close to Greenland's. In 1960, at what is very nearly the northernmost tip of Newfoundland Island, he found several overgrown house sites near a fishing village named *L'Anse aux Meadows*. The house sites were barely visible. All that could be seen of them were the slightly-raised shapes of what once had been walls. Even these shapes were overgrown with grasses and moss. It was immediately apparent to Ingstad that the building ruins were quite old.

Every summer between 1961 and 1968, Ingstad and other scientists quietly revisited these house sites. In all, scientists from five countries participated. A series of excavations were undertaken in order to see what could be learned of the people who had once lived in the houses.

In all, Ingstad, his archaeologist wife Ann Stine, and others, excavated eight house sites, four boat sheds, a smithy (where the occupants had made crude iron by smelting ore), and three large outdoor pits. Three of the sites were of the "long house" type—sleeping dormitories similar to several found and excavated in Greenland.

Among the important finds were a bronze pin that the Vikings used for fastening their cloaks, and perhaps most importantly, a spindle whorl of carved soapstone. The spindle whorl was useful to Viking

The excavation at L'Anse aux Meadows.

women who used it in spinning the thread that was necessary to make and repair clothing. Nearly identical spindle whorls had been found in Greenland excavations.

The finding of the spindle whorl was so important that the excavators started jumping up and down and hugging each other in celebration of the discovery. The spindle whorl proved that whoever the original settlers had been, they had not been the Eskimos or Indians who had lived in this area. The presence of the spindle whorl further confirmed the *Sagas* in their assertion that women and livestock had gone to Vinland. Without sheep to produce wool there would have been no need for spinning. And without women to do the spinning (spinning was regarded as women's work), there would have been no use for the whorl.

Another excavated pit at L'Anse aux Meadows.

The Vikings are often portrayed as heroic-looking conquerors.

Other things also pointed to Viking occupation. The native Eskimos and Indians neither smelted iron nor spun wool. Finally, though archaeologists did find a few arrowheads and other tidbits of evidence that Indians had been in the area, that evidence was minimal. According to Ingstad and his colleagues, had the Indians lived nearby for a longer period, the expedition would have found many more fragments of tools—chips of bone and stone. That there was evidence of some Indian activity was judged to be in keeping with what is claimed by the *Sagas:* Vikings met and traded with the Skraelings or native Indians.

Nor could the settlements have been built by fishermen at a much later date, since the nearby bay is too shallow to be useful to fishermen, and there are better places to fish nearby.

Most importantly, the expedition was able to use

a procedure known as carbon dating to determine the age of the spindle whorl, pins and other materials left by the occupants.

Twelve different readings were taken of L'Anse aux Meadows artifacts. All of them were compatible with the idea that the settlement was formed about the year A.D. 1000—in short, the time during which the *Sagas* claim the Vikings were in Vinland.

What does this mean? It means that in all probability a party of Vikings settled at L'Anse aux Meadows around the year 1000 and stayed long enough to need and build eight houses, use a smithy, a spindle whorl, and boat sheds. We do not, of course, know precisely how long that was. It might have been two years; it might have been ten. But if Ingstad's findings are correct, it means that the Vikings came to America about 400 years before Columbus.

Six

Who Saw the Americas Before the Vikings?

Opposite page:The carved head of a Viking chieftain, from the ninth century A.D. Did bearded men before Columbus inspire ancient legends among the Native Americans?

Helge Ingstad presented compelling evidence that the Vikings reached North America about A.D. 1000, precisely as the *Icelandic Sagas* claimed.

But the L'Anse aux Meadows findings suggest something else as well. If there were any pre-Viking voyages to the Americas, it will probably be difficult to prove they occurred.

The *Icelandic Sagas* were written down and made the search for Vinland somewhat easier than it might have been otherwise. The sagas gave scholars several clues. From studying them, for example, Ingstad was able to narrow the fields of his search by considering the different possible meanings of the term *Vinland*. With some general knowledge about Viking activity in the North Atlantic, his own theories, and modern technology, he was able to conduct the systematic search of the northeastern Canadian coastline that was ultimately successful.

Proving others came here before the Vikings is going to be more difficult, though, because historians have not yet turned up any reliable written records of such voyages.

Consider, for example, the case of the fourteenth-

century African king Abubakari the Second, who is said to have voyaged westward across the Atlantic, departing from the Senegambian coast in 1311. He may well have reached the New World, but he sent no one home to keep the story of his adventure alive. Nor did he leave any trace of his visit behind in the New World. He simply disappeared into the mists of history.

As for other visitors who may or may not have come ashore here, scholars are unlikely to find written records of their presence in the Americas. The cultures of the New World were basically pre-literate; that is, they lacked a written language. Of the many tribes in the Americas, only the Aztec and Mayan cultures in central Mexico had developed any form of writing by the time the Spaniards arrived in the sixteenth century.

The Erasing of History

Once there were many Mayan books in existence. If they had survived we might have learned a great deal about these early Americans. But a man named Bishop Diego de Landa destroyed them. The bishop was a Spanish missionary sent here to convert the Indians. Instead, his fellow Spaniards kidnapped and murdered their rulers and pillaged their cities in a bloodthirsty, unending search for gold.

"These people," wrote Bishop de Landa in the sixteenth century of the Mayans, "...made use of certain characters or letters, with which they wrote in their books their ancient matters and their sciences...We found a large number of books in these characters, and as they contained nothing in which were not to be seen superstition and lies of the devil, we burned them all."

Because of these book burnings there is a great deal that we do not know about the Mayans and their ancestors. We do know, however, that the Mayans were strongly influenced by the Olmecs, an earlier

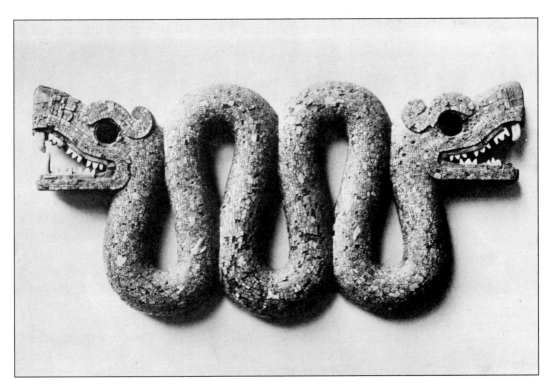

people from whom they learned the elements of writing and astronomy. Because many Olmec artifacts were found beneath Mayan ruins, we know that the Maya sometimes built their cities on top of Olmec cities. But if the Olmecs influenced the Mayans, who influenced the Olmecs? Some authorities believe the Olmecs were influenced by African visitors.

At the beginning of the twentieth century a team of archaeologists reported the discovery of a giant stone head made by the Olmecs. The site was called La Venta, in the Mexican state of Tabasco, about eighteen miles from the waters of the Gulf of Mexico.

In 1938, Dr. Matthew Stirling of the Smithsonian Institution began a series of intensive excavations near La Venta and rediscovered the huge stone head.

The spoils of war: this turquoise ornament, a double-headed serpent, is believed to be part of the Aztec treasure that Cortez sent to Emperor Charles V of Spain.

More than seven feet tall and weighing more than eight tons, the head was eighteen feet in diameter and had been carved from a single gigantic chunk of a stone called basalt. Immediately, those who looked at the head were struck by its thick lips, flat nose, tightly curled hair, and helmet. The face looked African rather than ancient Mexican.

Size alone would have made the carved head an awesome find. But two other things made it seem even stranger. First, since it had been fashioned from a huge stone and there was no similar rock for many miles, it was obviously transported with great effort from at least fifty miles away. It seems amazing that the Indians were able to move such a huge stone so far without the use of wheels. Second, perhaps the strangest thing about the head was its Negroid appearance. Historians had never found any evidence of Negroid people in the Americas. How could such a head appear so far away from Africa? No simple explanation seemed to make sense. Could the stone carvers have imagined every distinctive Negroid characteristic without ever having seen native Africans? Many thought not.

African Influences?

Scholars noticed that there was a great resemblance between the carved headgear of the stone heads and the helmets worn by men serving in the Egyptian-Nubian military in Africa about 700 B.C. The back of one of the carved heads showed Ethiopian-type braids. At first, historians assumed these heads dated to about A.D. 300, but carbon datings showed that the heads were nearly a thousand years older than that. In other words, they dated back to much the same time as the twenty-fifth Nubian dynasty (800 - 654 B.C.). Had black-skinned Africans visited America from Egypt a thousand years before Christ?

Ivan Van Sertima, a scholar interested in the pos-

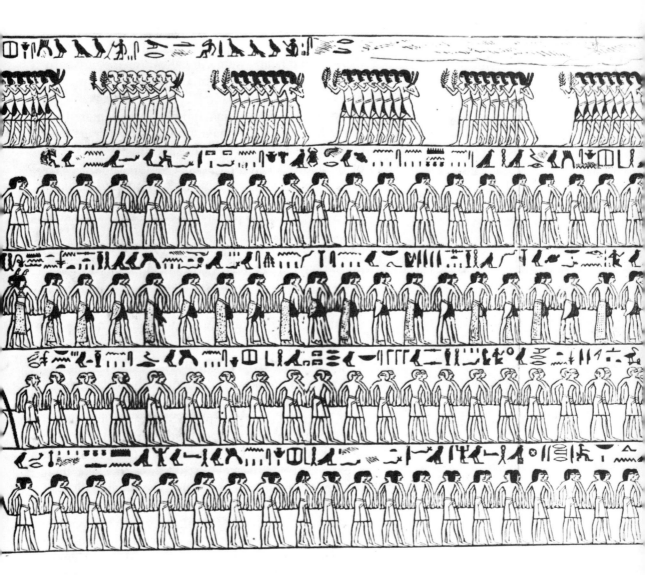

Some historians believe the ancient Egyptians, master architects of the pyramids, sailed to the western hemisphere. Are the similarities between the stone temples of the Old and New World due to Egyptian influences, or does stone masonry merely require similar building techniques?

sibility of African influences in medieval and ancient Mexico, believes it is possible that they did. At about the time the heads were carved in Mexico, a Negro-African dynasty had gained power in Egypt. The black-skinned Pharaohs in Egypt were hiring crews of Egyptian and Phoenician sailors. They ventured out of the Mediterranean Sea into the north Atlantic, traveling as far as Cornwall in western England in search of tin and other needed goods. Van Sertima believes such ships could easily have been swept into the powerful west-running ocean current between Africa and the Americas. They could have drifted or been blown by storms to the New World.

Other scholars are skeptical. Michael Coe, one of the leading American historians studying Mexico, argues that the stone heads were given broad noses and thick lips simply because the tools used to fashion them were too blunt to cut sharper noses and thinner lips.

Clues from Ancient Sculpture

Van Sertima, however, counters that many smaller clay figures made during the same period were also Negroid in appearance. Since clay is worked when wet, Van Sertima suggests that it can be made to look any way the artist wants it to. The ancient Mexican artists, he says, still chose to make their figurines Negroid. He notes the detail and realism of these small heads and believes that the artisans were trying to create portraits or likenesses of real people. Van Sertima's theory that the artists who made these objects had seen Africans is supported by a lecturer in art at the University of the Americas named Alexander Von Wuthenau. Von Wuthenau, an expert in the terra cotta pottery found in Central America, has amassed a large collection of these Negroid-like figurines over fifty years. "It is a contradiction to the most elementary logic and to all artistic experience that an Indian could depict in a masterly way the

Anthropologists look for physical characteristics between Native Americans, Pacific Islanders and Africans, seeking to trace the possible origins of the populations in the Americas.

"His beard could be long or short; trimmed or natural; pointed, round, or even forked and curled....In some instances, the Maya priests and other important personages, who could not grow beards themselves, would wear false beards in imitation of the divine founders of their religion."

Thor Heyerdahl, "The Bearded Gods Speak"

"Bearded faces could have been copied from bearded faces. Only the prototypes would have required living models. The plain truth is that while some of the objects carry a vivid impact, most of them look more like copies than portraits."

Geoffrey Ashe, *The Quest for America*

head of a Negro without missing a single racial characteristic, unless he had actually seen such a person," argues Von Wuthenau.

Though he has yet to prove his case, Van Sertima believes a small number of black Africans landed in the New World more than 2,500 years ago. He suggests that they stayed in central Mexico and bred with the natives, significantly affecting the Olmec way of life.

Yet no matter how closely African and pre-Columbian sculptures resemble one another, and no matter how much the pyramids of the Mayans resemble those built by the Egyptians, scholars must account for the navigational difficulties that would be experienced by any New World visitors. The Atlantic and Pacific Oceans are not lakes, but gigantic, sometimes treacherous bodies of water.

We remember, for instance, that according to the Sagas, Vinland was first discovered because Bjarni Herjolfson's ship was caught in a storm and blown off course on the way to Greenland. Of twenty-five ships that set sail for Greenland with Erik the Red, only fourteen arrived. The history of seafaring is always also a history of shipwreck.

The danger of navigation deepens the problem of finding America. If people came here from Egypt, Ireland, Japan, or some other country, how did they get here? Did they set out to explore the ocean, or were they caught in a storm and washed ashore? It is one thing to suppose that an occasional storm-tossed ship was beached in the Americas. It is quite another to argue that enough people came to influence a large culture of Native Americans. How likely is it that a dozen voyagers from Africa could have made an overpowering impression on an Olmec civilization of a million people? If Africans did come here then they must have come in numbers and they must have come with tools and inventions that the Olmec had not developed themselves. There must have

Famed Norwegian explorer Thor Heyerdahl has built many sailing crafts out of natural materials to test his hypotheses regarding the travels of prehistoric peoples from continent to continent.

been more than one ship. How many ships would it have taken? A dozen? A hundred?

Thor Heyerdahl, an anthropologist, historian, and navigator, has been widely celebrated for his attempts to prove that even before people had perfected written language, they regularly navigated the oceans. His dramatic and mostly successful voyages in primitive boats and rafts have gained him a great deal of publicity.

Prehistoric Sailors

Heyerdahl believes that adventurers traveled across the Atlantic and Pacific long before the Vikings or Columbus. He notes, for instance, the presence of carved figures with beards throughout Central America. Indians usually have little if any facial hair, so where did the figures with beards come from? Heyerdahl believes they came originally from Africa or Europe. He thinks these figures were imitated or copied by people in the New World, and then later transported west to islands in the Pacific.

Unlike other historians who do the bulk of their research in libraries and museums, Heyerdahl has proven himself an adventurer who is willing to test his theories at sea.

For example, in the 1950s Heyerdahl wanted to prove that the Indians of South America crossed the Pacific to the Society Islands. So Heyerdahl built *Kon-Tiki*, a small balsa wood raft on which he was able to make a 5,000 mile voyage from Peru to Tahiti.

A later Heyerdahl voyage strengthened the arguments of Van Sertima, Von Wuthenau, and those who believe that blacks came from Africa to South and Central America. Heyerdahl arranged for Africans to build him a boat of papyrus reeds. Experts said that these boats were intended for use on rivers and lakes and predicted that in the ocean the reeds would soon become waterlogged and cause the boat to sink. Heyerdahl thought that the boat

would do well on the open seas and in 1969 managed to sail *Ra I* from West Africa as far as the island of Barbados before having to abandon his ship. The next year, aboard a later, improved version called *Ra II*, Heyerdahl successfully completed his transatlantic voyage.

Inspired by Heyerdahl and others who have taken to the world's oceans in primitive craft, a man named Tim Severin sailed across the North Atlantic in a hide-covered coracle, very much like the one that might have been used by St. Brendan and other Irish adventurers.

What must be emphasized about all these voyages, however, is that they prove only that such voyages could have been made. They do not prove that they were made.

Thor Heyerdahl's papyrus reed boat *Ra II*.

Conclusion

Where Do We Go From Here?

We have noted that the Americas were inhabited for thousands of years before the arrival of Europeans. We have learned that the history of the Old World includes tales of explorers who ventured into the western Atlantic. We generally accept that at least the Vikings landed in North America before the famous 1492 voyage of Columbus. To honor the courage of the first sailors who dared the unknown Atlantic Ocean, we accept that Columbus "discovered" America. But when we say he discovered America, what we really mean is that—like no other voyager who may have arrived sooner—his landfall in the Bahamas and return to Europe the following year changed the world forever. No other ocean voyage has had such an impact on world history.

We have also learned that the Old World was not as ignorant of the seas and the lands beyond them as we had thought. An Irish monk named Brendan quite possibly set sail from Ireland in the sixth century. The sensational stories about his seafaring were told again and again throughout the middle ages, stimulating the imaginations of all those who heard them.

Then, too, there was Madoc. While Europeans

The New World, circa 1550. The discovery of the Americas by Europeans changed the shape and culture of the globe forever.

Vikings—the strongest evidence found so far indicates they were in North America before any other Europeans.

and their American counterparts liked to believe that this Welsh prince settled in America and helped create a race of "white" Indians, no reliable evidence of such a people exists. Nor has anyone ever turned up any evidence that Madoc ever arrived here.

Yet again, his legend reminded others that there might be lands in the western Atlantic Ocean. The stories of Brendan and Madoc kept the possibility of America alive for Europeans in the middle ages.

In Scandinavian countries the situation was different. Almost from the beginning, they claimed their ancestors, the Vikings, had been to America before Columbus.

Finally, in the 1960s, after a variety of false claims, hoaxes and an argument that lasted more than 150 years, Helge and Ann Stine Ingstad discovered evidence of the Viking presence in L'Anse aux Meadows, Newfoundland. Unlike the Kensington Stone and the Viking Tower, however, the Ingstad find was widely accepted by scholars from many countries. Carbon dating established that the artifacts uncovered by archaeologists in Newfoundland were nearly a thousand years old. The objects were made at about the same time the *Icelandic Sagas* claim the Eriksons began their journeys to and from a place they called *Vinland*.

Seeking evidence in the pre-historic settlements of North America is the job of archaeology.

Though Columbus showed the way to the New World, it was other explorers, such as Cortez, who gained the most fame and fortune from the Age of Exploration.

By now it would seem that we have reached a point in the discovery of America story where we can only await new developments. It is unlikely that any new discovery will be accepted unless it can also be backed up with written evidence similar to that presented by the *Icelandic Sagas.*

Yet the find at L'Anse aux Meadows—coming as it did after many false and disappointing claims—teaches us to have patience. It is even possible that future generations of Americans will discover proof that the Americas were first discovered by explorers who crossed—not the Atlantic—but the Pacific Ocean.

Who Discovered America First, and Does It Really Matter?

The answer is, yes, it does matter. It matters not just because we are curious about the history of the Americas, but because we have learned that the search for answers often provides us with new and unexpected knowledge. It matters because we know that nothing has improved the lot of man in this world like simple, applied curiosity.

It was the search of discontented and curious people that led the Vikings to discover Greenland and America. And if there is truth to the legends, a similar restless curiosity moved Brendan and Madoc to venture out onto the Atlantic. These stories kept alive the sense of wonder and adventure, not to mention the dream that there were rich lands to the west.

While people pursue the answers to a particular question, they very often discover something altogether unexpected. Columbus did not find the Indies. But he found something much greater, beginning with the knowledge that the world was not constructed the way ancient philosophers and saints had suggested.

The Columbus discovery brought home to people all over Europe a truth that men of the time were

Amerigo Vespucci, the lucky man who had two continents named after him—
North and South America.

already learning: that it is necessary and good to question popular opinion. In order to learn, we must take risks—just as Columbus risked sailing off the end of the world.

Columbus and his men were introduced to new foods, which not only kept them alive but improved their nutrition. These were just the first of thousands of life-improving resources and ideas that began to travel back and forth between the New World and Europe.

In the end, the most important thing about the mystery of the discovery of America is probably not who was here first, but something else: the new ideas and conditions that have stimulated people to think in new ways.

As long as humans remain curious about early American history, the search for answers will go forward. The solutions to this or any problem, gratifying though they are when we find them, are quite often less important than the search itself.

For Further Exploration

Geoffry Ashe, *Land to the West: St. Brendan's Voyage.* New York: Viking Press, 1962.

Frances Gibson, *The Seafarers: Pre-Columbian Voyages to America.* Bryn Mawr, PA: Dorrance & Co., 1974.

Gianni Granzotto, *Christopher Columbus: The Dream and the Obsession.* New York: Doubleday, 1985.

Helge Ingstad, *Westward to Vinland.* New York: St. Martin's Press, 1969.

Samuel Eliot Morison, *Admiral of the Ocean Sea: A Life of Christopher Columbus.* Boston: Little, Brown and Company, 1942.

Frederick J. Pohl, *The Lost Discovery.* New York: W.W. Norton & Co., 1954.

Ivan Van Sertima, *They Came Before Columbus.* New York: Random House, 1976.

Erik Wahlgren, *The Vikings and America.* New York: Thames & Hudson, 1986.

Additional Bibliography

Theodore C. Blegen, *The Kensington Rune Stone:
New Light on an Old Riddle*. Minneapolis:
Minnesota Historical Society, 1968.

John Stewart Collis, *Christopher Columbus*. New
York: Stein and Day, 1976.

James Robert Enterline, *Viking America: The Norse
Crossings and Their Legacy*. New York:
Doubleday, 1972.

Barry Fell, *America B.C*. New York: The New York
Times Book Co., 1976.

Eugene R. Fingerhut, *Who First Discovered
America? A Critique of Pre-Columbian Voyages*.
Claremont, CA: Regina Books, 1984.

Thor Heyerdahl, *The Ra Expedition*. New York:
Doubleday, 1971.

Edmundo O'Gorman, *The Invention of America*.
Bloomington, IN: Indiana University Press, 1961.

Index

About the Author

Though he's never been banished, become a monk, served a queen, or owned a ship, Renardo Barden has hoped somehow to find a new world anyway. While awaiting his big chance, he has lived in several cities and caddied on golf courses, washed cars, acted in small theaters, stacked boxes in potato chip factories, driven taxi cabs and trucks, delivered telegrams, started a typesetting business, and stuffed filing cabinets with his own writings. A graduate of the University of Colorado, he served as the editor of a martial arts magazine in California for six and a half years. He is the author of three earlier books, and lives in Portland, Oregon, where he writes about the visual arts and popular culture for newspapers and magazines in the Northwest.

Picture Credits

FPG International, 15, 16, 24, 32, 36, 53, 89, 99
Flying Fish Studio, 18, 34, 46, 63
Historical Pictures Service, Inc., 20, 23, 26, 43, 51, 100, 102
The Granger Collection, 21, 22, 68, 69, 79, 82, 85, 87, 98
Art Resource, 29, 39
Culver Pictures Inc., 35, 58, 60
UPI/Bettman Newsphotos, 42, 93
Reuters/Bettmann Newsphotos, 95
Mary Evans Picture Library, 45, 55
Mary Evans Picture Library/Photo researchers Inc., 48, 97
Minnesota Historical Society, 65
Newport County Chamber of Commerce, 72 (John T. Hope)
Yale University Press, 74
Helge and A Stine Ingstad, 80, 81
AP/Wide World Photos, 91